FRONT ROW BACK STAGE MARIO TESTINO

PAVILION

Foreword by **Suzy Menkes**
Introduction by **Anna Wintour**

FOREWORD

The rustle is like a breeze stirring among dry palm leaves. First the soft steps squishing on the plastic-covered runway; then the sweep of the program from the chair; the swoosh of Kelly bag stowed under the seat; the whisper of voices in the half-empty room.

Louder voices start to throw greetings across the aisles. Lips smack against twin cheeks. In their "pigpen," the photographers rumble and grumble, stiff joints cracking, lenses grinding as they are screwed into place.

POW! A deafening blast of music creates a wave of panic among the arriving throng. Only testing! The soundtrack recedes—just a soothing background to the buzz of gossip as the rows fill up. A battalion lined up at the back is waiting to charge the empty spaces.

Even the front row is no longer gap-toothed, as ushers check invitations against the handwritten names tied with white satin ribbons on to the inevitable little gilt chairs.

"No smoking," pleads the sign, hazy behind smoke drifting from hands grasping cigarette and pashmina shawl.

The room now looks like a giant carpet laid in a Berber tent. Black, black, black is the background color of all style nomads traveling between fashion capitals, but here and there is a splash of scarlet jacket; a lime ("It has to be Prada") sweater; a rainwashed sky blue ("That must be Marc") raincoat; and the season's pinks from marshmallow through peony, rose and fuchsia. A streak of lilac tints dandy socks and pastel Tod's loafers.

Ah, shoes! From each side of the front row, all you really notice are the feet. There are oony bare feet in poisonous patchworks of snakeskin sandal; pants puddling over vertigi-nous Gucci heels; stolid legs ending unexpectedly in saucy kitten-heeled pumps; and eather skirt hems butting thick-heeled knee-high boots.

Fashion editors who would die of embarrassment at finding themselves in the same outfit are bending conspiratorially over their neighbors' identical shoes, exulting in the joy of possession.

Feet are lifted in unison as the plastic is whisked from the catwalk. Lights down. Lights up! The volume of the music cuts the conversation in mid-syllable.

As the model steps out amid the flare of flashes, one front-row figure bends forward, trademark gleaming grin, a camera like a pirate's patch over one eye.

Mario is at work—stealing beauty and sealing it on film.

Suzy Menkes
Fashion Editor
International Herald Tribune

Marrakesh, March 1999

INTRODUCTION

What's always struck me about Mario, and what strikes me now, as I look through *Front Row/ Backstage,* is how much he adores fashion. Which is more surprising than you might think. It's amazing how many photographers I've worked with over the years who don't seem really to care whether they're photographing a T-shirt or a ball gown.

But Mario cares—a lot. He genuinely follows fashion: he's aware of trends, he recognizes style, he's always always on top of things. One of the delights of the collection each season is watching Mario maneuver through the crowd with his cameras. Because even though he doesn't take a million pictures, he seizes just the right moment.

The other thing about Mario that makes him special is that he absolutely adores women, which, needless to say, is a serious asset for a fashion photographer. But unlike so many photographers who are chameleonlike, he definitely has a "Testino-Girl." Mario does prefer a certain kind of woman—strong, self-assured, sexy—and usually wearing serious high heels. That slightly edgy Gucci girl is very much his ideal, although Carine Roitfeld and Camilla Nickerson also come to mind as quintessential Mario women. That apperciation of women not only comes through in his pictures but also helps explain why Mario is so good at discovering tomorrow's star models today. Certainly Georgina Grenville, Gisele Bundchen, Lisa Winkler Carolyn Murphy and, most recently, Jacquetta Wheeler wouldn't have the careers they have if not for Mario's sharp eye and enviable knack for capturing the look of the moment.

Another thing that makes Mario's work, of course, is the fact that he is not timid about eroticism—about a bit of sex in his pictures. But perhaps Mario's most serious asset is his phenomenal personality—also, in my experience, unusual in the business. People love to be photographed by Mario because he's so charming and funny and confident, not to mention so incredibly clever at seducing his subjects. So if he's shooting someone who is terribly famous, like Madonna, he can make her feel so at ease that she's not afraid to put herself and her image into Mario's hands. Because of his charm and his eye, he's also able to take people who are a bit stuck in a look that's stiff or dated and recreate them, much the way he has with so many models. Those unforgettable pictures he took of Princess Diana certainly stand out in my mind. Although we had seen a million pictures of Diana, we had never seen her looking so relaxed, accessible and modern as when Mario photographed her.

One of the things I've always admired about Mario is that he never overworks his subject. Some photographers are so controlling that they create a picture in their head before it's actually in front of the camera—which tends to produce a dead, or at least a flat, image; certainly, it doesn't lead to a lot of surprises. But while Mario is very efficient, very organized, and will discuss a shoot at great length, he is always spontaneous. Another thing Mario doesn't do is cut himself off from the world. He's out there. He enjoys life. You see him at restaurants, at parties, and at shows having a great time. You feel that spirit, that vitality and love of life in his pictures. Although Mario and I have worked together at American *Vogue* for only the last three years, I tried to bring him here fifteen years ago when I was Creative Director. In retrospect I think we were both a bit too young. We tried a couple of things, but it just didn't work out. Still, I followed his career very closely over the years. And since Mario knows how to charm, he always kept in touch—which was great with me.

I think in the last five years, Mario's work has really grown—from very good to very, very good. In fact, at this moment, I'd say there's no question that Mario is in the first tier of fashion photographers—the front row. From my seat, that's precisely where he belongs.

Anna Wintour
Editor-in-Chief
American *Vogue*

New York, April 1999

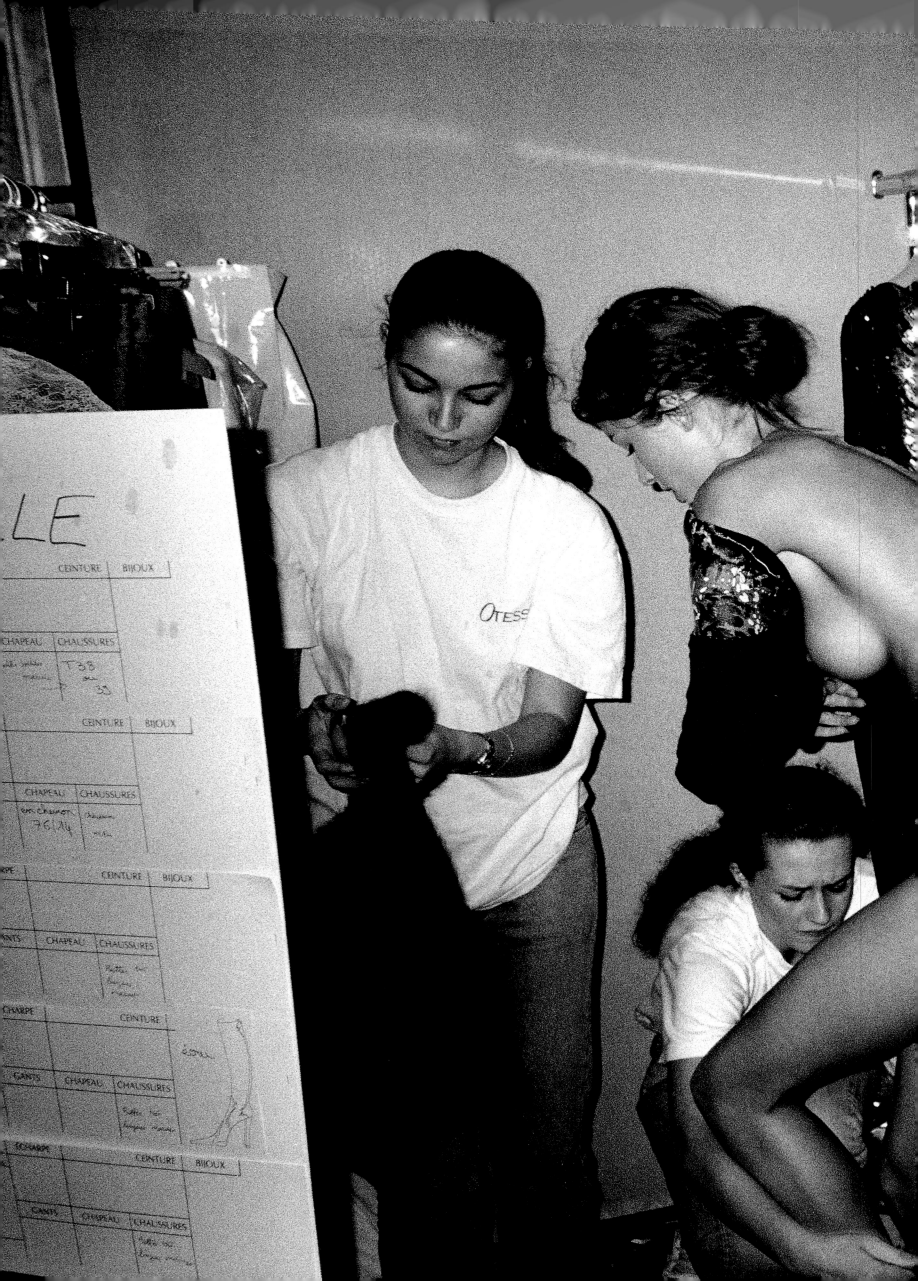

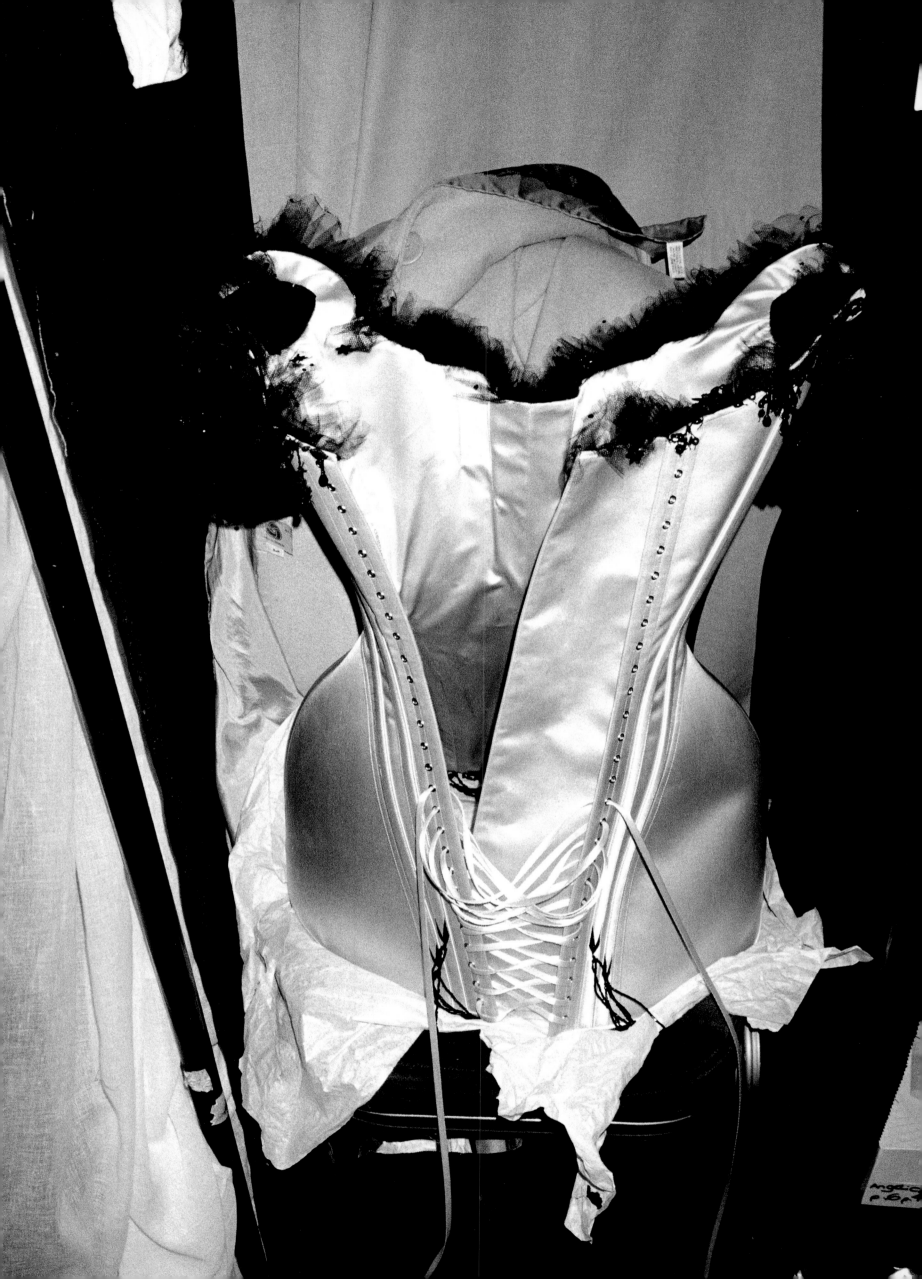

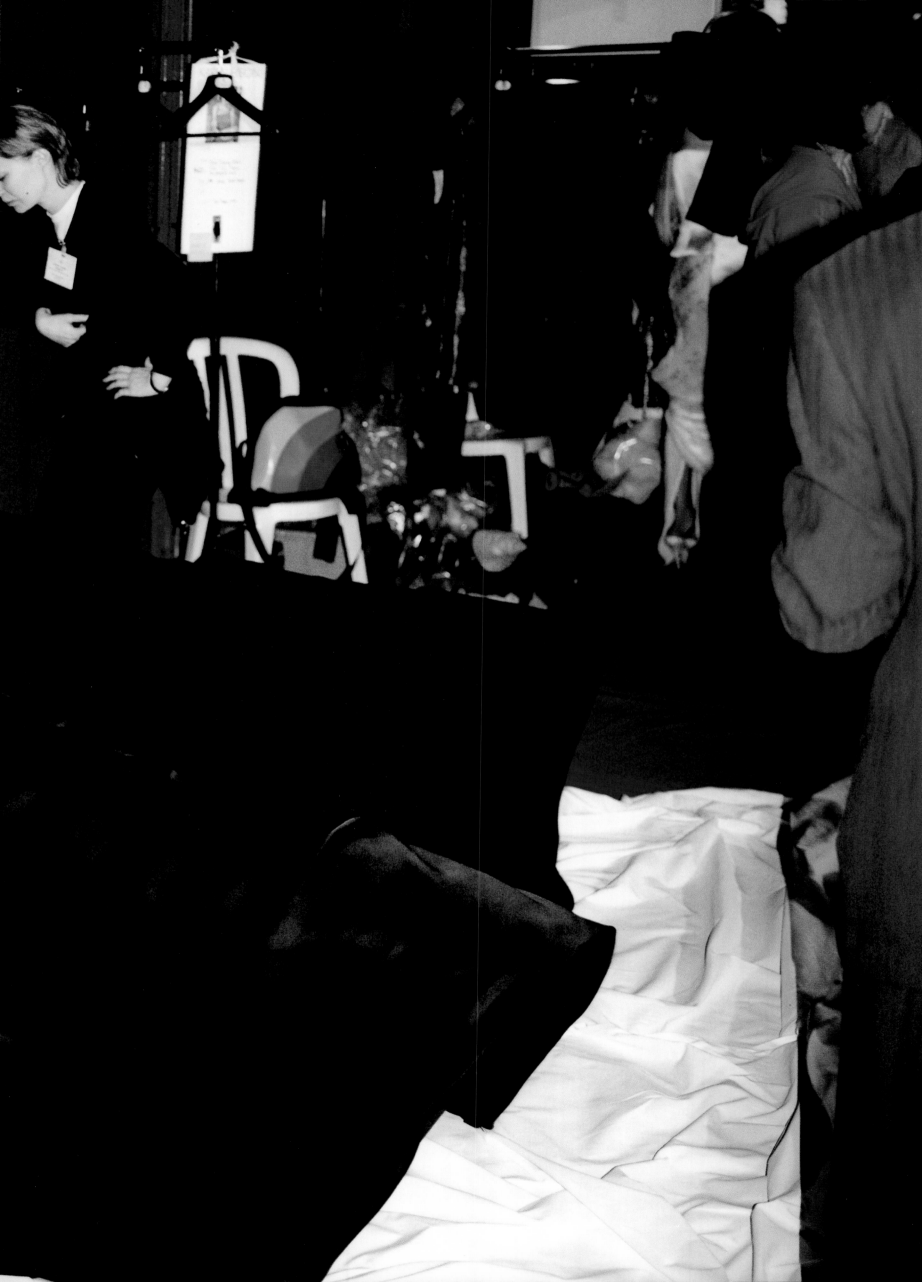

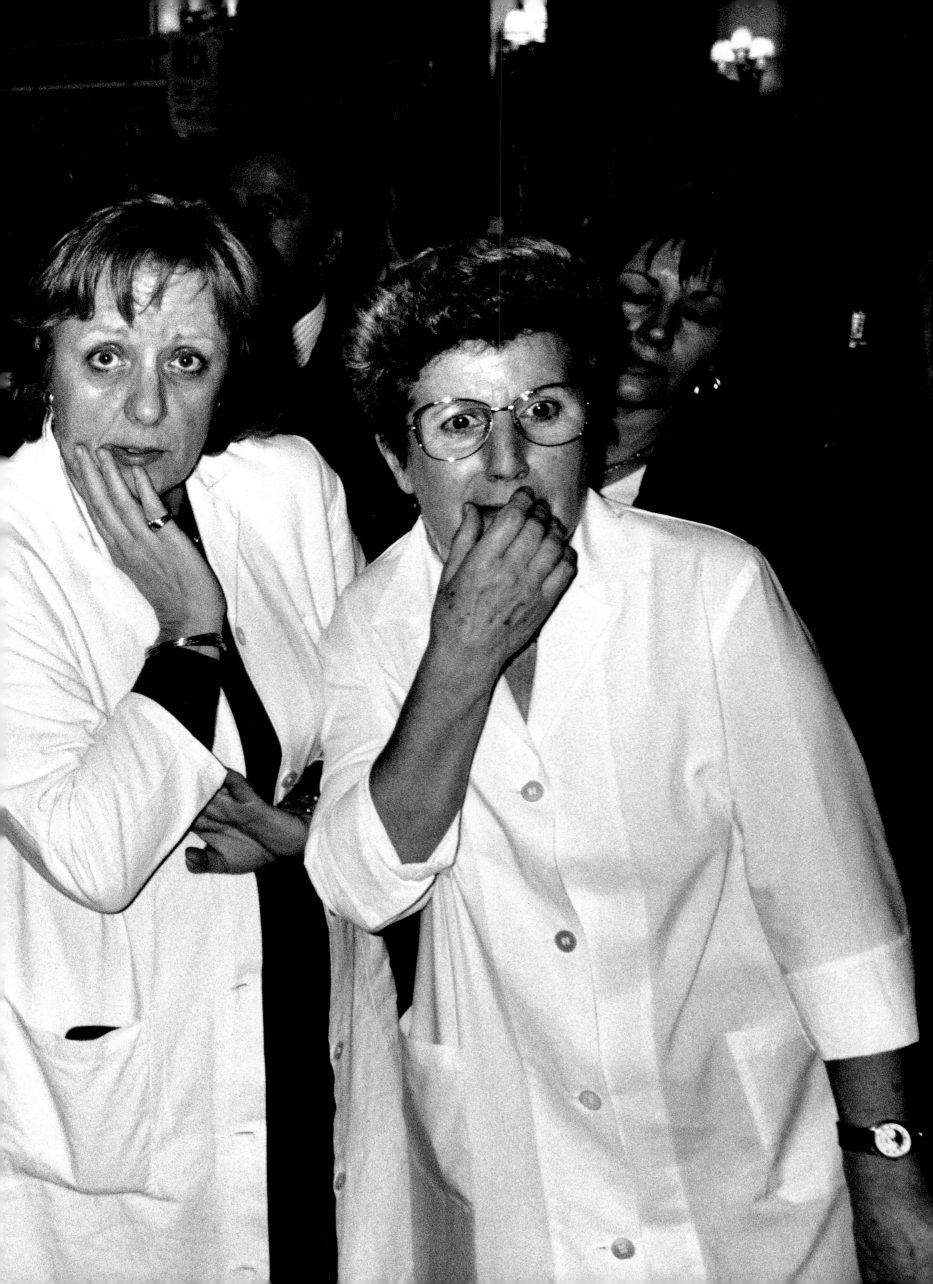

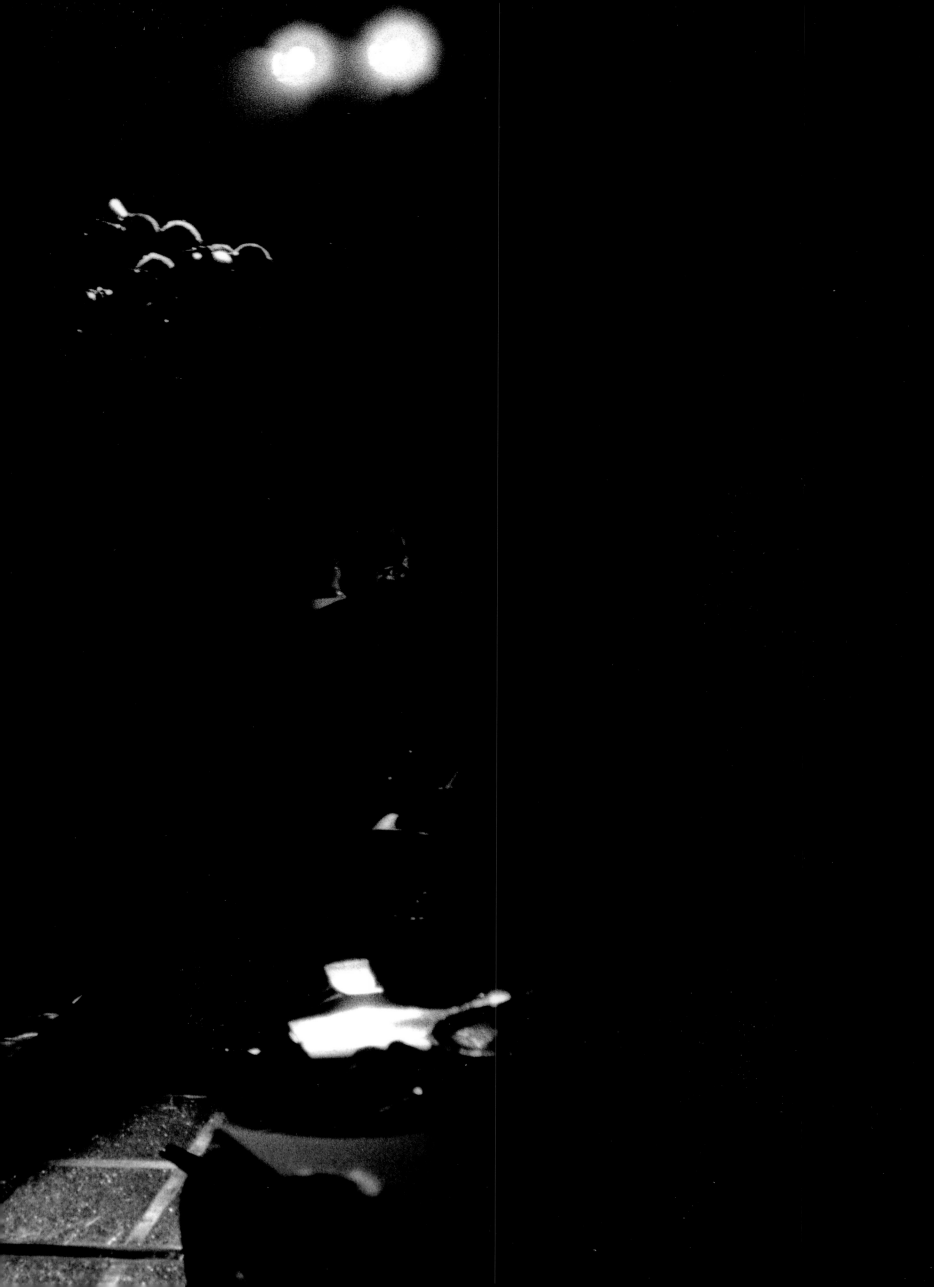

HAUTE COUTURE
GIVENCH

ACKNOWLEDGMENTS

My Mother and Father

Carine Roitfeld Eric Bergère Giovanni Testino
Antoine Agoudjian Emmanuel Anselmi Chris Arvidson Aurelia PR Andre Balazs Jocelyne and Jean Claude Bedel
Alessandro Belgiojosso Laurence Benaïm Isabella Blow Hamish Bowles Joan Juliet Buck Lucinda Chambers
Edibulga Chavez Mesh Chibber Sadie Coles ColorEdge Daylight Studio Dominique Deroche Gilles Dufour
Laure du Pavillon Heron Evers Victoria Fernandez Michele Filomeno Janet Fischgrund Greg Foley Tom Ford
Stephane Fusil Benjamin Galopin Jean Paul Gaultier Alexandra Geyr von Schweppenburg Terry Hackford
Anoushka Hempel (Lady Weinberg) Victoria Hennessy Michael Howells Marc Jacobs Stephen Jones
Ketchem Life Michel Klein Sandra Klimt Françoise and Christian Lacroix Karl Lagerfeld Salim Langatta
Nathalie Ledouarin Carol Judy Leslie Marc Lopez Marie Christine Marek Jake McCabe Stella McCartney
Jacqueline Menasakanian Suzy Menkes Camille Micheli Angela Missoni Michele Montaigne Youssef Nabil
Amber Olson Karla Otto Tom Pecheux Véronique Perez Orlando Pita Picto Loïc Prigent Jérôme Pulis
Gawain Rainey Umberto Raucci Tiffany Reed Stephanie Rutherford Nathalie Rykiel Sonia Rykiel
Carlo Santamaria Alexandra Schulmann Judith Schuster Ali Schwartz Raja Sethu Kevin Shalit Brigitte Sontag
Franca Sozzani Renata Strauss Giuliana Testino Girault Totem Philip Tracey Donatella Versace Blandine Viry
Matthias Vriens Neville Wakefield Adam Whitehead Anna Wintour

To the houses of Balmain Antonio Berardi Eric Bergère Chanel Chloé Christian Dior John Galliano
Jean Paul Gaultier Givenchy Gucci Calvin Klein Guy Laroche Julien Macdonald Alexander McQueen Missoni
Thierry Mugler Sonia Rykiel Yves Saint Laurent Jeremy Scott Martine Sitbon Valentino Versace Louis Vuitton
Yohji Yamamoto, and to all the other houses that have been so helpful in the creation of this book.

To the hair and makeup people for their creativity.

To the models, who never cease to inspire me.

To all the people who appear on the cover and the endleaves.

Special thanks to: Edouard Lehmann, Patrick Kinmonth, Stephen Gan, Christopher Scott Vann,
Quynh Mai, Huw Gwyther, Thomas Nutzl, Pietro Birindelli and Giovanni Zaccagnini

Edited by Edouard Lehmann
Art Direction: Stephen Gan and Greg Foley
Creative Consultant: Patrick Kinmonth
Coordinated by Christopher Scott Vann, Jake McCabe and Judith Schuster

This edition published in Great Britain in 1999 by
PAVILION BOOKS LIMITED
London House, Great Eastern Wharf
Parkgate Road, London SW11 4NQ
First published in the United States of America in 1999 by
Little, Brown and Company (Inc.)

A CIP catalogue record for this book is available
from the British Library.

ISBN 1 86205 374X

2 4 6 8 10 9 7 5 3 1

This book can be ordered direct from the publisher. Please contact
the Marketing Department. But try your bookshop first.

PRINTED IN GERMANY

**FRONT
ROW
BACK
STAGE
MARIO
TESTINO**

JOHN GALLIANO
Spring-Summer 99

CHRISTIAN DIOR
Haute Couture Spring-Summer 98

EXITING JEAN-PAUL GAULTIER
Haute Couture Autumn-Winter 98-99

CHLOE
Spring-Summer 99

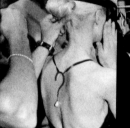

VERSACE
Spring-Summer 99

JEAN-PAUL GAULTIER
Haute Couture Autumn-Winter 98-99

MICHEL KLEIN FOR GUY LAROCHE
Haute Couture Spring-Summer 95

VALENTINO
Haute Couture Spring-Summer 98

CHLOE
Autumn-Winter 99-00

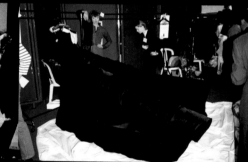

CHRISTIAN LACROIX
Haute Couture Spring-Summer 98

GIVENCHY
Haute Couture Spring-Summer 98

VALENTINO
Haute Couture Spring-Summer 98

CHRISTIAN LACROIX
Haute Couture Spring-Summer

CHRISTIAN LACROIX
Haute Couture Spring-Summer 95

VALENTINO
Haute Couture Spring-Summer 95

CHRISTIAN LACROIX
Autumn-Winter 97-98

BALMAIN
Autumn-Winter 99-00

JOHN GALLIANO
Autumn-Winter 99-00

VERSACE
Haute Couture Autumn-Winter

CHLOE
Spring-Summer 99

VERSACE
Haute Couture Spring-Summer 95

CHLOE
Autumn-Winter 99-00

PAUL GAULTIER
Couture Spring-Summer 98

CHLOE
Autumn-Winter 98-00

ALEXANDER MCQUEEN
Spring-Summer 98

ALEXANDER MCQUEEN
Spring-Summer 98

ANTONIO BERARDI
Spring-Summer 98

STIAN LACROIX
Couture Spring-Summer 98

VALENTINO
Haute Couture Spring-Summer 95

MARTINE SITBON
Autumn-Winter 99-00

CHLOE
Autumn-Winter 99-00

ALEXANDER MCQUEEN
Spring-Summer 97

JOHN GALLIANO
Spring-Summer 96

JOHN GALLIANO
Spring-Summer 99

JOHN GALLIANO
Autumn-Winter 99-00

JOHN GALLIANO
Spring-Summer 96

JOHN GALLIANO
Spring-Summer 98

YVES SAINT LAURENT
Haute Couture Spring-Summer 95

CHANEL
Haute Couture Spring-Summer 89

JOHN GALLIANO
Autumn-Winter 97-98

CHRISTIAN LACROIX
Autumn-Winter 97-98

ANTONIO BERARDI
Spring-Summer 98

VALENTINO
Haute Couture Spring-Summer 95

ERIC BERGERE
Spring-Summer 98

CHRISTIAN DIOR
Haute Couture Spring-Summe

CHRISTIAN DIOR
Haute Couture Spring-Summer 98

CHRISTIAN LACROIX
Haute Couture Spring-Summer 95

JOHN GALLIANO
Autumn-Winter 97-98

MARTINE SITBON
Autumn-Winter 97-98

SONIA RYKIEL
Autumn-Winter 99-00

ERIC BERGERE
Spring-Summer 99

PHILIP TREACY
Autumn-Winter 99-00

ALEXANDER MCQUEEN
Spring-Summer 97

CHRISTIAN LACROIX
Haute Couture Spring-Summer 95

YVES SAINT LAURENT
Haute Couture Spring-Summer 95

CHANEL
Spring-Summer 98

VERSACE

CHANEL
Autumn-Winter 98

CHRISTIAN DIOR
Haute Couture Spring-Summer 98

JOHN GALLIANO
Spring-Summer 98

STEPHEN JONES FOR GUY LAROCHE
Haute Couture Spring-Summer 95

CHRISTIAN LACROIX
Haute Couture Spring-Summer 98

CHRISTIAN DIOR
Haute Couture Spring-Summer 98

CHANEL
Haute Couture Spring-Summer 95

GUCCI
Spring-Summer 98

GUCCI
Autumn-Winter 99-00

GIVENCHY
Haute Couture Spring-Summer 98

YOHJI YAMAMOTO
Autumn-Winter 98-99

GIVENCHY
Haute Couture Spring-Summer 97

JOHN GALLIANO
Spring-Summer 99

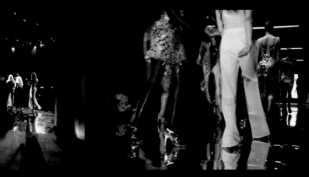